Portraits Of A Broken Soul

A Collection Of Introspective & Reflective Poems

Rachita Sahay

Made with ❤ on the BookLeaf Publishing Platform
www.bookleafpub.in
www.bookleafpub.com

Dedication

*I dedicate this book to the little girl who always
dreamed of becoming a poet.*

Acknowledgement

As I close the final chapter of this journey and share these words with you, my heart overflows with gratitude for those who have been my unwavering stars and gentle anchors.

To my family, you have been my safe haven through stormy days. Your unwavering support has been the lighthouse, always guiding me through the fog, shining brightly when I needed it most.

To my grandfather, whose memory is like a guiding star in my night sky. Your wisdom and warmth have been a constant, gentle presence, lighting my path with every step I take.

My brother, you have been the sun that warms my coldest days, filling my heart with a boundless joy that never fades. Your love has been the comforting embrace that has kept me grounded through every twist and turn.

To my husband, you are my compass and my cornerstone. Your unshakeable strength and unwavering support have wrapped me in comfort, offering warmth during every challenge. I truly appreciate and love you more than words can express.

A heartfelt thanks to my therapist, whose wisdom has been the gentle rain nourishing my growth. Your guidance has helped me heal and clarity in the midst of life's storms.

To Archie, my furbaby, you are the joyful heartbeat that dances through my days. Your presence is the pure, unconditional love that brightens every moment, making it more meaningful.

And to you, dear reader, thank you for embracing this book and helping me realize my dream. I hope these pages provide you with the warmth and solace you seek, as your support brings my dreams to life.

With all my love and deepest thanks.

Preface

Dear Reader,

If you've found your way to this book, it's likely because you're seeking a place of solace, a quiet companion to walk with you through your own journey. As I set out to write these poems, I was searching for a way to release the many emotions that had quietly built up inside me. These pages are a heartfelt expression of my own experiences with self-exploration, reflection, and the intricate tapestry of life and relationships.

This collection was born from a deep, personal need to find peace amidst the chaos of my own struggles with depression. It is a mosaic of moments spent grappling with anxiety, finding my way through recovery, and exploring what it means to be both a writer and a person in the 21st century. Each poem is a fragment of that journey, crafted to resonate with those who have faced similar challenges and seek understanding and connection.

The path to creating this book was far from smooth. There were days when writing felt like an insurmountable task, each word emerging through a veil of physical pain and emotional turmoil. Yet it was on those very days that my vintage typewriter—my reward for perseverance—became a comforting presence. Its rhythmic clatter was like a warm embrace, reminding me why I had fallen in love with writing in the first place.

I am profoundly grateful to those who have stood by me through this journey. To my grandfather, whose memory is a soft, enduring light in my heart; to my parents, whose gentle love has been a constant source of strength; to my brother; to my beloved Mahi, the heartbeat of my life; to my husband, my unwavering pillar of support—each of you have shown me what true love and healing feel like. Thanks for being my cup of coffee at the beginning of each slow day and the end of each hectic one; to my therapist, whose wisdom has guided me through countless epiphanies; and to my Shih Tzu, Archie, whose companionship has been a boundless source of joy and comfort. Each of you has played a vital role in this journey, and for that, I am deeply thankful.

This book does not follow a rigid structure, reflecting the natural flow of my thoughts and emotions. The poems within are woven together in a way that mirrors the ebb and flow of personal introspection. The tone is a blend of reflection, melancholy, raw intensity, and occasional glimmers of hope, crafted to offer both comfort and connection.

Dear reader, if you've chosen to delve into these pages, know that I understand the path you walk. It's a journey filled with its share of challenges, but also moments of profound clarity and connection. I hope these poems offer you a sense of companionship and warmth, much like a comforting cup of coffee or a heartfelt hug.

Thank you for allowing me to share this journey with you. May these words bring you solace and a sense of belonging.

With warmth and gratitude,

The Painter

I sit at the ledge,
arms reaching out, grasping
the canvas, so blank,
white as a foggy cloud

reflects nothing but lack
or my wasted potential.
I sit with a crusty, limped paintbrush
that doubts its own ability.

Desperately holding my withering palette,
the paint dusts off like sand,
in the haunting quiet of
my endless desert.

I self sabotage, or pacify,
they seem alright don't they?
I stare at puddles of red and blue,
there's so much more I could say

I see through the blur,
a table of fir,
with paints and potions,
oils and varnish.

Too tired to squint to see better,
even without the effort,
I know it's all I need
for my masterpiece.

I stay motionless, defeated,
crying comfort, hoping it's enough.
a voice seethes, shaking its head,
"You're lying to yourself."

Startled, I look around to see
my own thoughts now a stranger's voice.
my back now aching,
even from reaching the canvas.

The palette and brush leave my grasp,
crash at the ground poetically,
too tired to pick my broken pieces,
the voice pulls me out to a void.

Am I on an astral plane?
I see through the bird's-eye view,
the hunched body, battered and bruised,
staring lifeless at the void canvas.

my wrathful and embarrassed gaze
turns to a sympathetic sigh,
the wear and tear on the body
exposing unnoticed battles I fight.

I scream, deafening screams,
cheers or morbid cries,
the voice in her head,
her only part now alive.

Waiting to be heard,
hoping she'd reach
everything she needs
for her masterpiece.

Morning Mayhem

My tranquil sleep
Turns to face the windowsill;
The sunlight peeps—
Chaos slips in for the kill.
My serene slumber
Pins in my head and sorrow.
I turn and twist and lumber,
Promise my body a better morrow.
Once the golden burns through my eyes,
And in my ear the bluebird sings,
I cherish my unforeseen prize—
The daylight no longer stings.
My somber soul or wrecked mind.
Perhaps the Devil wakes on my shoulder,
Till the Mighty drifts me back to light.
A piece of me still smolders—
That will forever be my plight.

The Golden Cage

A gilded butterfly flutters,
Perched in a frail glass cage;
Fingers tap at an old typewriter—
This being her only escape.

Palms against the pane,
A cloud of raspy breath;
She peeks into an endless enclave,
Soft sighs of realisation.

She weaves through the hours,
Checked lists to keep sane;
Four corners of a sanctuary,
Watering flowers of the mundane.

Caught in the dance of corners,
Spins around in a maddening daze;
Hands trace familiar edges,
Trapped in the labyrinth's maze.

Muddled in sweet delirium,
Surrenders to the veil of delusion;
Finds solace in her glass aquarium—
At least it grants vision to undreamt dreams.

Bones To Ashes

And when they put me to rest,
Burn me, bone to ashes;
Bury the whispers deep in my chest.

As specks of flame rise,
Like glistening teardrops
Falling from heaven's eyes.

It's your perfume,
Enveloping my body,
My soul exhumed in smoke.

It's your laughter,
Buried in my bones—
He, my master.

It's your touch,
Traces along my broken skin;
My heart, I clutch.

It's your reminiscences,
Cigarette-burned Polaroids,
Sepia-toned keepsake instances.

It's your skin,
Bruised and tattered in silk—
Traces of where you've been.

At last, when they sear
The remnants of me,
Make sure they only
Burn the bones, the nails, the teeth.

Foolish soul,
Even they carry your reveries,
But keep me
In echoes, for your heart's glee.

The Poet's Sanctuary

Nestled by the windowpane,
Crying in comfort or pain,
As the clock strikes seven,
She lingers by the typewriter.

Unfinished thoughts claw
At the white polished keys,
Each fading alphabet
A witness to a story told.

Cloudy days and rustling leaves
Knock at the window—
Golden summer days,
Melt into soft, molten rain.

Coffee cup stains
Taint the virgin page,
White as a widow,
Quiet as a ghost.

Click of the keys,
Click of her thoughts;
The black ink stains,
Murmur secrets to the page.

Ink bleeds from her heart,
Pouring onto the parchment—
Ones she'll never breathe—
Forever etched carnage.

Amber hues creep,
The warm glow diffusing
To embrace the blue
Of the quiet night alluring.

The golden wax, once firm,
Falls like moonlight rain—
The only witness, a silent confidant
To threads of thought spun into secret tales.

As the moon claims the sky,
The paper letter drenched
Like a soaked rag
Or bleeding canvas.

She locks her sanctuary,
Sentinel of her secrets;
The only key is her mind, fortified
Until another quiet midnight.

Survive

Check for a pulse,
Revive, revive—
Plead and wail
To a fragile thread of life.

Ghost of a heartbeat cries,
Ears pressed to my chest;
Fingers grasp my bloody vein—
She won't survive.

A lifeless frame in gentle repose,
Grief drapes the dark room;
Specks of sunlight
Touch her face with weary hope.

An internal battle she fights,
At war with her own mind,
To carry on for her beloveds,
Torn apart by relentless strife.

Casket's mellow embrace apprised,
Tears haunt the room;
Screeches of her mother's howl
Plead to bring her back to life.

"I'll stay," she whispers in compromise,
Letting go of the bony hands;
Wakes gasping for air—
The Grim painfully sighs.

The Albatross

Hangs around my neck without a fret,
Feed on my soul, clings like regret;

I hear the screeching sound of its voice
Whenever I dare to step foot into the light.

Hangs around my neck like lingering pain—
My trembling feet won't make it to the end of
the
Of the tunnel, each effort in vain.

Hangs around my neck,a chapter unfinished;
My weary breath, the light of my eyes
diminished.

Hangs around my neck like a noose—
I struggle with it; should I tighten or let
loose?

Hangs around my neck like a warm
embrace—
At last, I surrender, welcoming fate with
grace.

Bottle On A Shelf

Bottle on a shelf, forgotten,
was once the finest fruit, now turned rotten.
not the kind you'd sip, but ruined.

Once a reward of passionate pursuit,
covers itself with a warm blanket of dust
the shine once beamed, now dull rust.

It silently sits, deluded, a prized possession,
doesn't know its long lost, forgotten.
like a royal robe, it wears deception.

Faded labels, gold edges diminished,
once an emblem of grace, now vanished,
lingering in the shadows, tarnished.

What was once a vessel of laughter and cheer,
sits in the dark, its purpose unclear,
Realisation dawns, bringing forth a tear.

a remnant of joy, now withered decay,
sparkles of gold, fading to grey
in essence, a muse of yesterday.

It awaits its turn to once again shine,
for when the hands rediscover its light,
hopeful or foolish, you decide.

Kintsugi

I trace my fingers over the scars—
The jagged skin, love parched.

It feels the warmth of my touch;
Gently, my fingers brush.

Her pain, her sorrow—I'm so alone;
I carry this burden on my own.

Sobs into the pillow, her painful cry;
I stroke her hair until it dries.

Slow lumbers of women on the street—
I match their pace with a gleaming greet.

A smile that echoes words of praise;
She struts away with a confident gaze.

My mother cries laments of her days;
I hear with pain, my heart ablaze.

I lay her in my lap, a peaceful child;
Give warmth and caress stifled cries.

Broken spirits, glasses, and poisoned weed—
I piece together like Kintsugi.

For all I see in every broken soul
Is a peeking reflection of my own.

Metamorphosis

Enclosed in a warm embrace,
Threaded cocoon in lilac lace,
Cradled in the comfort of a womb,
Oblivious to the concealed tomb.

Melting down in puddles of stagnancy,
Blind to the impending exigency;
Covered in dust,
Maddened by lust—

Of comfort and solace,
Only a warm bed, a freezing palace;
Feet frozen in place,
Sloth's dizzy embrace.

Bougainvillea weaves malicious threads
Over bare feet as it spreads;
Too timid to move,
Too indecisive to choose.

The cocoon lies withered, drought, lifeless,
Walls closing in, breathless;
Shrunk in its own skin,
Consumed by its own sin.

As comfort turns to misery,
Self-loathing fades to pity,
A small crack breaks—
A long gasping breath it takes.

From the hollow rift, hues spring,
Pushing through, unfolding its wings;
The moth exhales a relieved sigh—
Shedding its nest, ready to fly.

The Shapeshifting Reflection

I stand facing a silver pool,
a woman draped in pearls and jewels.
I stare in profound fascination,
a glowing, shapeshifting reflection.

Is it me?
Or is it a child,
with a crinkled nose and gleaming eyes,
dreams intact, neat pigtails,
muddy from the backyard, gazing at
chemtrails?

Is it me?
Or is it my newfound youth,
knowing now of life's harsh truths?
Her face no longer lit with innocence,
She's discovered the weight of self-awareness.

Is it me?
Or the girl I was at 23,
with hollowed eyes and a broken smile,
far exceeding her own great expectations,
Still battling doubts and reservations?

Is it me?
Or now a woman at 33,
with a baby she adores?
Pleading to heal all wounds, self-implored,
shoulders slumped, baby at the breast,
her inner demons seeking rest.

Is it me?
Or a woman crinkled and old,
Her face a testament to life's stories told,
eyes a window to memories held,
wishing her youth could be gilded in gold?

Is it me?
Or is it my ghost,
an outline of features once loved most,
wishing she had loved herself more,
hauntingly beautiful, like an old painting
restored?

Reaching to grasp my face in her hands,
wailing in a ghostly screech, "Live while you
can."
A crack in the mirror breaks my trance,
or is it life offering me a second chance?

The Train That Takes Him Home

Echoes of the steam train,
a pavement with glistening rain.
he gushes through the crowd to catch
the train that takes him home.

Hands bruised, face fought war,
broken edges of skin, soul like tar.
tired and aching, to rest in his mother's lap,
he jumps on the train that takes him home.

A lost poet, a singer, and everything in
between,
gazes out the window, all the thing he
could've been
grips at the pane, seething through pain,
on the train that takes him home.

He lets go of the bottled up cries,
a pool of emotions draining his eyes
self-loathing, self-soothing, still berating,
on the train that takes him home

the mask fall off, on the floor it cracks
off the slumped shoulder, fall the sacks
of lost, regret, remorse and guilt
on the train that takes him home

As darkness yields to dawn's embrace,
a soft relieved sigh lights up his face,
soothingly the station bells sing to receive,
the train that took him home

Conversations With The Moon

Each night she strolls,
sits by the empathetic fig tree.
The dim-lit glow of the lamp
offers warmth and welcomes.
The moon, her quiet confidant,
questions of life and its sorrows.
Revelations of the darkest thoughts,
confessions: *I often think of ending it,*
silenced by the bustle of the river.
Sighs, sorrows, regrets, and laughter—
tales revisited on quiet midnight walks,
guided by the soft silver glow.
The river crashes against the shore
on tales of laughter.
The breeze offers a gentle caress
on tales of sorrow.
As the morning hues peek
from behind the mountain peak,
The moon tucks her secrets away
in cradles of its dark shadows.
Until another night, she bids farewell
to her quiet confidant.

The Memory Box

I found an old box I kept,
Chipped wood, rusted edges,
Engraving diminished by time's soft blow;
Lock clicks open with a soft ache.

Small odd trinkets wave hello,
An array of oddly beautiful keepsakes,
Each tarnished by the touch of time,
Reciting tales and lullabies.

A button with a bear,
Childhood's prized possession;
A clay turtle charm,
Courtesy of an old friend.

A bow with frayed edges,
Pins now patina'd;
A ticket with numbers fading,
Life's first carnival.

I stare with loving fascination,
Me, the collector of old things.
I laugh at life's metaphor:
Broken things love broken things.

I search for beauty in cracks,
Completion in imperfection.
The musty box stares back at me,
Like a naked truth.

Grew up reading poems of Plath,
My innocence half-understood it,
Tainted by a feeling unknown;
It followed me to my adulthood.

Tracing the spines at a bookstore,
My hand stumbled upon *The Bell Jar*.
I saw my reflection peeking,
Some words a mirrored plea.

A familiar ache etched my soul,
Dwelling deeper in a feeling unknown.
I wouldn't have made it—
Am I making it now, though?

My heart always ached for Monroe,
By day, a visage of gleaming grace,
By night, a hollowed, haunted face—
Similar pain, similar plight.

Bustling through wild city lights,
Trying to make it,
Bound by incomparable sorrow,
Aching arms, longing to leave a mark.

Intrigued by art, I studied Van Gogh;
Painful realization, I see the scheme—
I could've eaten yellow paint myself
If it made the suffering stop.

Life's irony mocks my fate:
Broken people make beautiful things.
When aches of life consume us,
We pour the love outwards, if not within.

I snap the box shut, an unexpected memory
road,
A hopeful thought glimmers in my mind:
Kintsugi's art, golden seams—
When I first saw the cracks repaired,
something healed within.

The Rain's Serenade

My heartbeat quickens,
panic rising with my breath,
a storm brewing in my chest

I stumble out the door,
gasping for breath,
running into nature's embrace.

Thunders resonate,
like the thoughts in my head;
the sky lets out a growl.

A violent breeze,
like the storm in my chest,
I desperately search for solace.

Dark clouds shroud,
the sky breaks down,
unburdening the heavy tears.

each drop strikes like tender blades,
purging my skin and body,
cleansing my burning flames.

my body is drenched
in the rain's embrace,
I let it soak my sorrows.

The chilling wind,
a whispered balm,
wraps my battered body.

I breathe in the muddy air,
the petrichor envelopes my soul,
healing what no one broke.

The storm's roar,
now a serenade,
its hymn a holy chant.

My body purged,
I find reprieve,
my spirit redeemed.

The Black Robe

In the quiet corners of my early days,
my tiny fingers wrapped around his,
holding on for strength when i could barely
find mine,
gentle as God, strong as a rock.

Every morning, I'd stare fascinated,
as you got in your mighty black robe,
to fight for justice or to save the world—
it all meant the same thing to me

Sweet promises, always fulfilled,
a child's reckless demand, your highest
command.
You'd come home with dolls and candies
all I waited to see was your glasses on your
crinkled nose.

Fate had other, cruel plan,
took you from me, leaving me speechless—
too innocent to understand the greatest loss
of my life.
I bear the burden as an adult of a broken
child.

I carry you around like a ghost,
the smell of cigars or French cologne,
my soul as black as your dark robe—
doomed, for a love like yours I'll never know.

for every time in despair,
I thought of thoughts too dark to ink,
I felt the same hand on my head—
I sobbed into the arms of a phantom.

I will carry you around forever, to keep
like a souvenir you cherish,
never to be forgotten, memory etched
till I'm gray and join you at the gates of
heaven.

Archie

In the quiet of the afternoon,
when the gloom reaches it's peak,
gently watching the quiet monsoon,
a companion my soul seeks.

It meets your quiet wide eyed gaze,
brimming with a childlike gleam.
They light up my darkest days,
with pure joy, you beam.

Soft fur, a pillow to my aching soul,
tail wags, my happy serenade.
Healing my wailing heart, makes it whole,
deciphering your little charades.

Little paws, soft imprints,
patch my splintered heart.
Gentle gaze and a selfless kiss,
my God-sent counterpart.

In each quiet moment shared,
as storms of life unfold,
your presence, a comfort declared,
a love unspoken, untold.

Forbidden Love

The summer I first met your gaze,
I quietly felt my heart implode.
a heart untouched by love
suddenly caught in a web of the forbidden.

the fire in my heart was hard to keep—
silent beneath my rose-flushed eyes.
They judged me in hushed tones,
pointing fingers as I passed.

Whispers turned to snide remarks,
narrowed gazes and snickers.
foolish, fantasied, or both,
"She's caught in the web of want."

My only sin was wanting him,
desiring what they all coveted.
The weight of this love I bear,
casting stones upon my heart.

They called it profane
and threw judgments like knives,
cutting through like a winter breeze
against a wilting rose.

Time's old wicked tale—
wrong place, right time.
the audience screams, "What a mess,"
sabotaging it with all their might.

"It's a whimsical tale," they say,
spun from silver threads.
they don't see the scars it leaves
or how deeply my heart bleeds.

but away from all the chaos,
In a cottage beyond their reach,
flourishes a golden rose in silence,
fortified by a bell jar.

What once was scarred
now rests in mesmerizing tranquility.
What was stoned to near death
revives beneath true love's tender kiss.

It thrives in whispers of sweet nothings,
its roots nourished by passion.
Its leaves, green and glowing,
blessed by the sacred.

In a field beyond good and evil,
free from judgments and jury,
their union sealed in the pages of time,
in a forest where the hummingbirds sing.

The Trial Of Torment

My soul hollowed, I could no longer hide.
Battered and bruised, I surrendered.
Forsaken, I whispered, "I'm in pain,"
and a council convened to dissect my anguish.

They painted my life's portrait,
as if they were the artists of my fate.
"Too young to be so sorrowful," they said—
surely, they must know better.

For every battered breath spoken,
they dragged me to a courtroom.
Judge, jury, Judy, and Carol,
clutching their pearls, disappointed.

Flatline white walls, shadow-draped,
a room filled with acquaintances,
with pitchforks and stones to throw—
my jury out before my foot touched the
ground.

Snarling gazes, murmurs under breath,
condemning eyes char my body.
My fearful gaze—am I in Salem?
My once-white gown, now bloodstained.

For every cry, every appeal,
I sought a judgment of validation.
"Blasphemous—she's too young,"
I sighed, sinking deeper into desperation.

And when the mundane became unbearable,
declared sloth, insanity, or sadness,
my mind protested in critical ways,
enslaved by opinions and scrutiny.

Announced guilty of seeking gaze,
they shackled me with chains
of life's burdens and hoaxes,
sentenced to a quiet death.

Dragged away like a murdered carcass,
they look away from their masterpiece.
Confined in the shadows, like ugly truths,
I bid my time, awaiting my demise.

Chained

Drowning in the dark of the night,
I gaze longingly at the starless sky,
a void I long to succumb to,
crying prayers to a lifeless statue.

the heart, a fractured mirror,
reflects the face of a lover,
word too bitter for his cold touch,
webs of lies from his slithering tongue.

Arms gripping her fragile skin,
pools of tears or blood,
conflicts with her own mind—
Do I deserve this?

My boredom, a slow-burning flame,
quietly consuming my sanity.
My tired hands polish the routine
of my life, too scrubbed to shine

A ship lost at a violent sea,
yearning to crash into the waves,
for its pieces to softly give in
and settle peacefully to the ground.

A lighthouse catches my tired gaze,
my mind torn at odds,
was I looking for it all along?
Guilt creeps in, followed by a hesitant sigh.

A man draped in grey,
his eyes, vast and endless,
deeper than the void I wished
to succumb my breath to

His voice, so achingly gentle,
his skin, molten gold,
a fire, she fears consume her,
his hair, black as the night's embrace.

Each word spoken,
a lifeline cast into the abyss,
each promise,
a balm to her battered heart.

strangled in the shadows,
he is her only salvation,
the North star beaming now
in a seemingly starless sky.

Chains of another, gripping her flesh,
each step taken towards light,
tightens and snarling at her neck,
a bond forged in deceit.

Hissing threats and ugly lies,
her heart torn in torment.
Sawing mercilessly at the rusted cage,
he repairs every night.

And so she lingers,
at the edge of night and day,
tendrils of darkness wrapped around her,
as the sun bathes her in sympathy.

She waits beneath her starless sky,
prisoner to her own desires,
longing for the crack of daylight
to cease the endless night.

The Coffee Shop

I sit at this ivory table,
my paper as white as it is,
in this quiet coffee shop
my thoughts melt into a puddle.

Craving comfort in cradled corners,
the aroma of the brew—
the only company I keep,
finding solace in muted conversations.

I trace moments of my reflections
in the dark, swirling cup,
dark as strings of thought in my head,
exchanging glances in solitude.

The world outside, bustling,
time dances a slow waltz here.
For when the world crumbles shamelessly,
these hushed walls stand as a regal fort.

People watching, stories and dreams—
I gaze longingly at they unfold.
am I the ghost from *Funiculi Funicula*
who sat unfazed as the coffee grew cold?

As my ink flows onto paper,
my mind now sacredly quiet,
the coffee cup leaves its mark
a smudge of hushed glory.

The Alien

I wake at half past the
break of dawn,
my curtains half-closed,
sky peeking.
The dawn stares at me—
lazily, I stare back.
The curtain, an eyelid
tired, half open, trying—
cosmic mimicry of my
struggling restless soul.
The blue-grey threads
reach out from the windows
like tiny little parasites,
glowing, growing, intertwined.
They tickle the bottom of my feet,
merging, holy union
crawl through my entire body,
taking over the vessel.
My blood, once poisoned,
my feet that would always ache,
illuminated by the parasite
a white, alien like glow.

The lost fire in my loins
burn neon blue for life.
My stomach's lost appetite,
burnt up, revived, famished.
My chest, knotted in heartache,
consumed wholly by the Holy Ghost.
My throat, too tired to squeak,
whispers prayers of gratitude.
My eyes, half-awake,
shine brown, blue tears pool.
My mind, once grey matter,
radiate the illuminated light
And I rise with my hair like fire,
my body possessed, elevated—
the day after I almost gave up,
my body stood resurrected.

Don't Save Me

My purple prune lips
My ivory cracked eyes,
My tongue too big to swallow—
My own selfish pride
I reach for the bottle again,
The Red Cross skull, no surprise.
my locks of flowing brown,
save my last ounce of honour,
they keep hidden between
my tortured, haunting eyes.
My skin slowly turns morning—
Blue sky, no room for mourning.
I plead oh mother, father, & husband,
I beg you brother, don't cry.
For this isn't a demise,
just a bab put to rest. Kindness—
forever sleep, my only reprise.
Resting hollow, porcelain doll,
torn seams and edges alike.
please don't try to save me,
Not this time, I cry.
My big toe, a small white thread—
Etched in red, do not resurrect.

Silver Pool

A liquid silver pool,
Unclaimed forest ground—
A puddle or a lake,
Sheen, sheer sunlight.

Passes through, absorbed,
Thoughts and reflections alike.
The white oval ivory stares,
Hopeful, profound eyes.

Baby hair locks fall
Beneath the silk hairband
To caress her baby face—
Carnation for a mouth.

Frozen in chains of thought,
She whispers to the ground.
The silver pool puddles,
A ripple or a response.

They exchange no pleasantries—
Just raw, unnerving doubts,
And hopes, and broken dreams,
Without a single sound.

And when the dusk hits,
The canopy of tree leaves
Too shy to touch each other—
The mirror or the treetops.

Bid a soft, relieved goodbye—
Both hearts, now lighter, fly.
She glances one last peek
At her soulful confidant.

Flower

And there I was,
barren brown ground
raw, tantalising earth,
a red fleshy flower
or a newly open wound
who could tell?
For the world to gaze,
and with blades dissect.
I bled and bled,
As the laughed and mocked.
I bleed and perform
in the desert stage,
I, the bloody disco ball
for the world to see.
I looked around to see
my cuts bleeding through.
one thing they can't take
is my flickering light soul.
And so, I fold inwards,
Neatly putting my petals
Back into place, I stick—
Careful caterpillar mastermind,
Inwards I weave.

My open-book self, I fold—
Inwards, to protect.
Bitter, cliche, or closeted,
You better decide.
For I choose peace until I fly
away from the desert, butterfly.

Fine

Sad Monday morning,
I am in mourning.
Ah, my lover is dead,
Killed in cold blood,
By my demands and logic.
Oh, he was just fine,
but now he sits,
heart and soul frozen cold,
As I beg, plead, and plead for mercy.
My heart deceived,
he mocks my sadness,
and hones his truths.
I shiver at every pitch,
I cry at every sigh.
My heart is sorrowed,
begs to differ and die.
it's truly beaten, battered—
wants to say goodbye.
But Wendy, Linda and Rene,
they all want me to be fine.
the priest, the in-laws, and jury,
they all want me to be fine.

My mother, father, & brother,
they all want me to be fine.
My best friend Judy & Esther,
they all want me to be fine.
My gods and goddesses,
they all want me to be fine.
My own weak heart and cries,
they all want me to be fine.
My coaxing, lying husband—
they all want me to be fine.
They know not so,
that the push me forward
to a world unprepared, red crown,
Face, red clown. I slant backwards—
you push me anyway. Burn, burn.

Sand

I was always
so worried of losing
grip or my destiny—
held you close to me,
clutched on for dear life.
Gripped it like golden sand,
and so it crumbled
away from me, grain by grain,
floating down like fairy dust
or molten golden lava.
Time took you away,
piece by piece, grain by grain.
I stood frozen, clutching,
foolishly trying to outrun
the wicked ways of time,
as it took you away from me.
And all I was left with
was a clutching fist,
a broken and battered heart,
and forever red eyes.

Tess.

Tess wears black,
mourning or hiding,
little cautious steps—
she dares be defiant.
The foot of her heel
crushing grasses,
or dreams, unclear.
Struts to the carriage,
feet jump reluctantly,
her eyes uninviting,
meets Sir Alec's bidding,
dives down the alley.
Her eyes, frightened,
grips the coarse wool.
His face, terrifying,
she pushed distraught,
caught in the charade.
She reigns hell, fighting.
Curse the carriage,
the horse unsure,
nights defensively.
Tess's eyes, volcanic rage,
sees too red to understand.

It's not the carriage,
but the road that leads
to a tall, dark tower home—
a church-like penitentiary,
the graveyard of her dreams.
She lashes the carriage,
wrath of her fury,
embers to flames,
engulfing them alive.
The death and destruction
of the infantile mind—
should've jumped ship.
The simple survive.

Longing

I never knew longing,
it seems fascinating,
to long for someone,
to have your heart ache
for the touch of him.
I never knew guilt,
till my heart was burning,
sobbing and aching
for him, but I'm promised
to another, I long for his
sweet words and kind touch,
contrary to your lashes.
I long for the shivers, when
I cried, contrary to your
huffs and sighs and slamming
doors when I broke down.
I long for his letters,
checks upon me, flowers.
I long for the long hug
goodbyes, contrary to how
you left me at the skeleton house,
which had no life, I peeked

out the balcony; the colours
now faded ten tones lighter.
a hope flickered, my nonchalant
heart thought it's a dream.
but the longing and guilt
consumes me like a wildfire,
every time you touch me.
I feel his warmth, his skin,
for his heart was gold, yours cold,
oblivious to my tearing skin,
too rigid to crumble when I
fall to the depths of my
wounded despair, he picked
pieces of my soul to stitch,
put me back like a tapestry,
only to hang and catch dust.
For the most haunting part of
it all is, they were both you—
just in different phases of
falling in and out of love.

The Wake

The teardrop shattered,
hit the cold concrete,
synonymous to your heart.
haunting silence screeches
soul vacuumed black hole.
Switch flipped, face frozen,
last drop, turned to ice,
reaches to meet my lamenting
heart once warm spring field.
frost-bitten, unrepairable cracks,
I let out a last dying wail.
All warmth, leaving the ship.
You looked the other way,
distraught, despairing, and eager.
my blood trickled too slow
for your taste; you wait—
your rage storm, hurricane,
passed through me, white noise.
stood in the eye of the storm—
a speck of my bone still,
waited for you to look back.

It waited, waited, and waited
for 3650 days, salt air
I exploded into find glass mist—
my blood and matter stain
your white shirt, I once adored.
Your frightened eyes, bloodshot,
open wide in unbearable pain.
Grasp and try to catch
the fragments of me, fading away.

Love

His towering frame,
lowered to kiss my,
forehead as he promised,
"I believe I'm in love with you."
She looks up, innocent,
beautifully prepared,
smirks at the suntanned
"You don't want to, trust me."
For I am ember or ruby,
Burning yet precious.
I am the force of nature,
rain and hurricane alike.
I am an engulfing volcano,
mesmerising but could char you.
I am the ethereal cloud,
soft summer rain and lightning strikes.
I am the 4 a.m. coffee,
comforting and bitter, electrifying.
I am the glazed golden sun
bask in it, don't stare too long.
I am the Renaissance church,
the supper and crucifixion.

I am the needle, dope—
the high shooting through,
burning veins and overdosing.
I am poison or euthanasia,
humble relief and harrowing regret.
I am painted blue, Picasso—
mesmerising yet melancholic.
I am the poetry of Plath,
beach read or Lady Lazarus.
I will reside in every corner
where your red blood flows,
and I will smoulder to make
warmth and room to sleep.
I will haunt you, forever
to keep and seek.
I will destroy you,
in the most heavenly divine,
For I am on earth.

Pool of gold

And in the bare middle
of the endless blue,
rafts and rigorous ocean,
reaching out to touch my feet.
The pool of gold collapsing,
molten hot lava falling to meet
the soft bed of ocean sand,
Splashing its gold liquid,
spilling over the crashing waves.
Shies away, blind blue cloud,
puffs its chest, so proud.
The pool of gold now dead silent,
only till the hour of dusk.
The truth revealed, plot unkind.
will the sun blind my soul,
or will the clouds hold my honour?
Impending doom soft cries,
cinematic view, dramatic endings.
My blind soul, blinded eyes,
all anguished paradise.

Sea of diamonds

The white glittering sea
pool of mercury
liquid platinum gold,
cutting through coarse
sand shun ablaze.
Pool of white wave,
cracks and patterns they make,
caressing the molten brown.
Little beads under my toes,
red freckled sun kist nose.
Curling flutter butterflies,
sepias sunflowers, white noise,
vintage Kodak film patina'd.
Witness black roll, confidante,
keeper of secrets sleeps
in the back of fringed suede purses.
Ocean wave blissfully hums,
waves through my ear stun.
My resting red eyes,
run cuts and bleed from sandstones.
The pigeon makes its way proudly,
shamelessly to my sinking body,

gnaws and bites with its beak,
into my soul, it peeks.
Dark deep soul sobriety,
the upside down entirety.
White sun, dark purple skies,
eyes shining white light beams,
soul sunken, barren widow.
Tall wooden Victorian window,
an innocent victim peeks,
her will to live she seeks.
Hands touch lightning electricity,
Neon-pattern skies over the city
of ghouls and priests and judging olds,
the clutch their pearls.

a brown mushroom cloud, neon soul,
nuclear shining, cunning to the core,
sets the city ablaze as she breathes,
the blackout awoken by morning sun.

She

Maroon painted nails
grabs the backrest
pine wood chair,
peacefully empty.
Now she rattles,
the drag screeches
as she sits facing me,
dark, somber eyes,
seldom evil,
an all knowing smile.
Hard to keep her
throbbing gaze,
confrontational look.
The pine chair sits
peacefully in my company.
Her maroon long nails
dig & rattle the backrest.
The drag screeches mercilessly,
she sits on her throne,
dark somber eyes, ever knowing smile,
look at me confrontationally.
I pour tea, broken teapot,
my unwelcome guest commands.

The steam rises to greet
the air of unease.
The mystic fortune teller,
her dark crystal ball,
fiery red amethyst,
reflect my worst fears.
Her tender fingers graze
the back of my hand,
my skin slithers and burns,
flinches but can't recall.
Eyes ghastly white,
possessed by thoughts,
strapped to her deadly chair.
Uncalled for electrocution.
Pens down on torn papers,
morbid prophecies.
Her hand bleeds tirelessly,
words marked by blood.
She smiles, accomplished.
My brain now fed full
by snarling, compulsive thoughts,
arrogantly letting go of
my burnt, bruised hand
that barely survived.

She smirks, pushing
the broken chair in place,
turns her back to leave,
tucks her tendrils.
she bids goodbye,
although, only until next time.
Religion is what you believe it is.
He screamed, bloody in his eyes,
Sacred lands, lamenting planet.

Switch Flip

My mundane Mondays,
directional chores of
everyday chaos.
I hear the bustle,
indistinct conversations,
ever-present white noise.
When it hits with force,
damning sonic wave,
apocalyptic silence surrounds.
The weight settles in,
my depression seats itself
arrogantly on his chair.
As the weight sinks,
its bloody teeth deeper
into my shoulder skin.
My swift steps,
now hunched, deadly drags,
my tired body around,
floating like a cursed ghost.
My sunshine smile,
now a forced curt
greeting to mask
the inner conspiracy.

The edges hanging
by a delicate thread,
bleeding edges, stringy skin,
holding fortress together.
My radiating joy,
now diluted by agony,
dissolving my will.
my words of wisdom,
now berating thoughts,
lashing lashes, bleeding back,
masochistic woman,
blood dripping down,
my bending, breaking back.
I stumble, fall
backwards, resting my will
to survive, to be alive,
sinking into cold comfort
of tar filled concrete
one with my obsidian soul.
The edge of my lips
forces a soft smile.
I cannot fall further.
My only knowing comfort.

Wings Of Glass

My wings of glass,
glued pristine and mighty
to my worthless hunched back.
its luster frightening,
emblem of my potential,
flickering flame, burning bright,
never steady, crisis existential.
dark room, soft glow of light
cuts through clouds like sword,
on a good day in flight.
A wave rising high,
only to crumble before the shore,
melts like cheap wax,
every time it gets too close,
the glimmering sun's tax,
melting, wasted, disposed.
He sits on the cliff edge,
questioning its worth,
the wings mending for fledging,
boon or a curse, the rebirth?

Alice

I often felt like Alice,
falling down the rabbit hole—
depth of my own despair,
dark abyss of my mind,
tumbling, snapping bones
as I hurl down the
treacherous path,
thoughts poking like
pine needles, scratching my
brain on the downfall.
Hushed whispers, "She's lost it,"
stoned for being aloft.
I've stood at the stake
and been stoned from the crowds,
been the archer,
been the prey, leaping
out in the dark forest—
self constructed labyrinth.
I feel up familiar walls,
desperate hands
running out of breath.
the soft grass, snarling now,
turn into snakes.

I tumble again,
no reality to catch me.
This time, land on
the poisoned pitchfork,
my lifeless eyes.

Who are you?

Who are you?
When the door shuts,
and you sit in silence
with nothing but
your own company,
self-basking glory—
the only sound,
your own breathing.
Who are you?
when you sit by the window,
shut the cab door,
the hustle of the city
now fading into white noise.
You put your earphones in,
as you sink into
the ragged upholstery,
gazing out at
the cemented landscape
as you escape.
Who are you?
When you are in the kitchen,
lazy Sunday afternoon,

baking a lime pie
to calm the buzz
In your own head—
who are you?
When you sit at midnight,
the dim light of the night lamp,
the only source of light,
as you pen down these thoughts,
raw to the bone,
to dull the ache in your chest
who are you?

Winter Flower

It all started that November,
when the shade of your blue shirt
matched that of my melancholy.
the street light seemed too bright—
I squint my tired, teary eyes.
The smell of winter flowers,
envelopes my wallflower soul.
I wasn't looking for love,
did my eyes wander secretly?
Conspiring in great unison
with some well-wishing divine force
because the heavens rained from above,
drenching in gold, my lifeless soul.
I tried to shrug off the signs,
Like moonlit dust of my shoulder,
how my face fit perfectly well
in your hands— so gentle, I longed
to be held with such warmth,
or how words deemed unnecessary
for our quiet conversations,
or how your touch was the blanket
my shivering soul prayed for.

My desperate eyes searching meaning
found its tunnel light
In the smouldering glow
of your kind eyes.
I placed you on a sacred pedestal,
slowly turning into an obedient believer
to a faith I passively dismissed.
The universe looked down at
His holy masterpiece,
smirking proudly at his grand scheme.

The Monster Under My Bed

He lurks under,
the smocked mattress crest,
my timid bed frame,
the ceiling above his abode.
Dark, musty floor—
the bed that houses
his tall, lanky frame,
slimy, bony ribs
rest on the cold floor.
His claustrophobic world
lit up by my nightlight.
he lives in rage and fear
burdened by my nightmare,
a soul that came to haunt.
He stares, black in his hollow face,
my piercing gaze penetrates
his void black, sinister eyes.
the monster saw death,
the soul haunted him back.
Unexpected scrutiny—
now he lives submissive,

hiding from the tar-black soul,
too heavy to comprehend.
He dare not gaze at her,
creeping into corners,
awaiting release, quiet escape,
prisoner to a lawless god,
he bides time, counting sheep.

Will To Live

I woke up facing left
the world weighing on my chest.
I open my eyes, a small peek,
my will to live, I seek.
My tired eyes ponder,
my feet touch the ground, in wonder.
I lift my shoe to peek,
my will to live, I seek.
Dragging feet make it to the mirror,
eyes squinting, rub them to see clearer.
My piercing gaze slowly peeks—
My will to live, I seek.
I wash my face & sins,
My head heavy falling, sharp pins
Pain shut eyes, inside peeks—
My will to live, I seek.
Heavy monster lounging like a sloth,
Daily mundanes, fold my cloth.
Gaze into the TV, tired peeks—
My will to live, I seek.
Gaze out, still scenery,
Dull blue sky, tiresome greenery.

Longing for the sky, I peek,
My will to live, I seek.
In infant smiles, kind eyes,
haunting laughter, sad goodbyes,
in my memory box I peek,
My will to live, I seek.
In shadows, endless ocean,
dark thoughts, my quiet devotion,
Into the black abyss I peek,
My will to live, I seek.

Monster

Dark, musty room,
creeping corners,
air dense with pain,
pools of mercury
stand 10ft tall,
arrogant as a king,
ghastly contrast
to my shivering
peasant frame.
Screwed sharp teeth,
gnarly, nasty growl—
low rumbled, my stomach.
Piercing gaze in the dark,
quickened, raspy breath,
silent heart palpitating,
all-consuming entity.
blanket of cold tar,
claws gnaw mercilessly,
chewing on my brain.
bloody pool, pungent tears
stain my hollow face.
The monster ablaze,

mighty, wretched fire,
self-stricken match,
engulfing me, my potential,
all-consuming catastrophe.
fingers tear through
broken flesh, snapping bones—
crawls out of me,
my own bloody womb.

The Eternal Duel

Hill on clifftop side,
Two rocks, unlike,
Sit as two silhouettes,
Facing the facade.

Sunlight paints gold
The landscape, new & old.
One turns to face
The other, eye locked in gaze.

She asks, infantile,
"What do you wake up for?"
His eyes lock with that of the sun,
Narrow gaze, spirit stirred.

He snorts, smirks uneasy,
"To live a life," he scoffs.
Her eyes study, careful,
She sees a small crevice.

To an infinite galaxy,
Dark thoughts and stars alike,
He, looks away to hide
Any broken seams.

Her turn to lock eyes,
Of the golden sun crystallized.
The ember brown of her eye,
Sunkissed kind smile.

"I wake to live too," she announces—
It meant two different things,
He understood well, yet
Asks inquisitive, aware.

She points her slender finger
Direction of the golden pool.
"Just like the sun lives to nourish,
The tubelight just to light.

The moth lives to sacrifice
His worthless soul to the pyre.
For love stands taller
Than his might or his life.

How the ocean touches the feet
Of the sand, his mistress to keep."
Yet the man scoffs and snorts,
His arrogant, prude eyes.

His seams half torn,
The galaxy pool's black thorn
Bleeds out of his tortured soul.
He's grasping desperately.

He mocks her innocence,
"Oh, stupid, foolish child."
Comes to the aid of the scorpion
Who might as well eat her alive."

And that's the difference, oh mind,
She smiles as she sews his seams.
I have loved and been loathed,
You might as well eat me alive.

The heart, she sobbed,
Wailing desperate cries.
the mind's will shattered,
Thorns coat his thick skin.

Her satin sheer skin,
Cuts, bleeds crimson seams.
The thorns slice open,
Her heart or her wounds.

The mind wailed helpless,
roaring hateful cries.
The sun hides, a cloud blanket
Thundering dark cries.

The green grass cliffside,
Pooling with red blood,
And his tar-black light
Reach to meet and hide.

As heart and mind ponder,
Locked gaze, eye to eye—
Eye of each other's storm,
Always destined to find.

For each lifetime loop,
Parallel realities alike,
The mind and heart face
A game with no prize.